930
MATCHBOOK
ADVERTISING CUTS
OF THE TWENTIES AND THIRTIES

Edited by
Trina Robbins

DOVER PUBLICATIONS, INC.
Mineola, New York

Publisher's Note

The twenties and thirties are generally regarded as being a golden age of commercial art. Bold, inventive graphics were churned out in such volume that it is amazing that the quality of so much of it should have been so high. And some of it appeared in unusual places. One entire genre involved advertising art for book matches. All surfaces, inner as well as outer, were liable to be covered with advertising. Trina Robbins has been able to assemble this collection of matchbook advertising from many of the best examples of the period.

Bibliographical Note

930 Matchbook Advertising Cuts of the Twenties and Thirties is a new anthology, first published by Dover Publications, Inc., in 1997.

DOVER *Pictorial Archive* SERIES

Library of Congress Cataloging-in-Publication Data

930 matchbook advertising cuts of the twenties and thirties / edited by Trina Robbins.
    p.   cm. – (Dover pictorial archive series)
    ISBN 0-486-29564-8 (pbk.)
    1. Matchcovers–United States–Miscellanea.   2. Decoration and ornament.   3. Clip art. I. Robbins, Trina. II. Title: Nine hundred thirty matchbook advertising cuts of the twenties and thirties. III. Series.
NC1890.U6A15   1997
741.6'94–DC21
                                                    96-40194
                                                     CIP

Manufactured in the United States of America
Dover Publications, Inc., 31 East 2nd Street, Mineola, N.Y. 11501

DESIGNS FOR EVERY CANDIDATE

STAND BY OUR PRINCIPLES of DEMOCRACY

VOTE FOR

CLOSE COVER FOR SAFETY

No Entangling ALLIANCES

The People's Friend

At Your SERVICE

Your VOTE & INFLUENCE Appreciated

You Will Be More Than Pleased

⊗ VOTE FOR

It's a Grand & Glorious Feeling to be an AMERICAN

Defender of the Constitution

Re- ELECT

HONEST CAPABLE FEARLESS

A Republican

Untouched by Scandal

AMERICA for AMERICANS

VOTE REPUBLICAN

1

DESIGNS FOR EVERY CANDIDATE

REPUBLICAN
GOP
YOUR VOTE & SUPPORT APPRECIATED

VOTE
REPUBLICAN

HONEST
EFFICIENT

Your VOTE WILL BE Appreciated —THANKS

The MAN for the OFFICE

Our Country!..
RIGHT
or WRONG
..Our Country!
STEPHEN DECATUR

GOD BLESS AMERICA
We are proud to be
AMERICANS

BAD NEWS,
GOOD NEWS,
COME WHAT MAY
WE'LL ALWAYS
BELIEVE IN THE
U.S.A.

God Bless
AMERICA
LIBERTY EQUALITY JUSTICE

It's a
Grand & Glorious
Feeling to be an
AMERICAN

DESIGNS FOR EVERY CANDIDATE

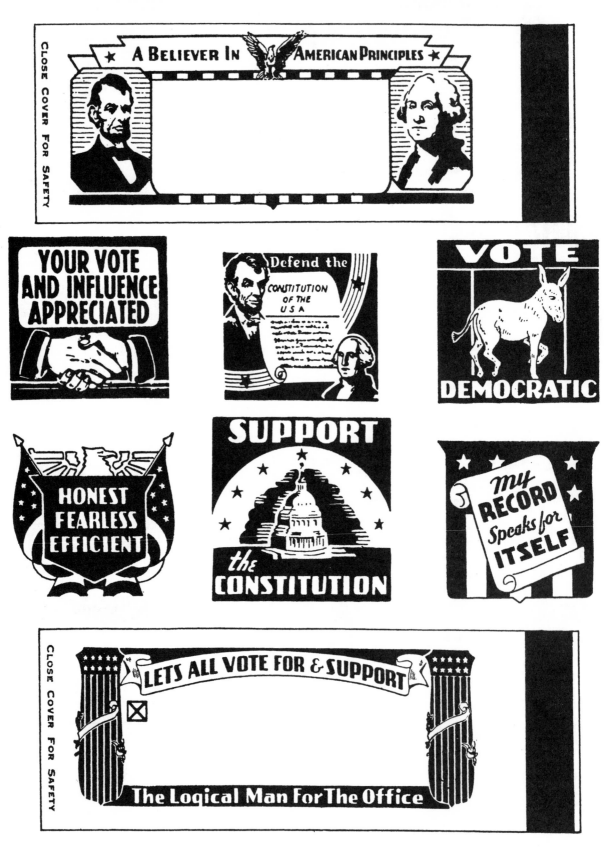

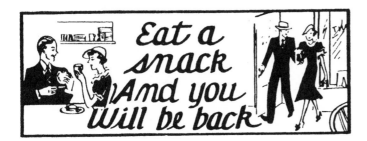

OUR *delicious* COFFEE "HITS THE SPOT" SHORT ORDERS & SANDWICHES OUR *Specialty*

Good Things to EAT

Table Service

Dee-licious COFFEE

Golden WAFFLES WITH BUTTER & SYRUP

The Best- Coffee in town

Grill and TEA ROOM

SANDWICHES AND COFFEE

Tasty Toasted Sandwiches

fish fry every friday

CHOP SUEY

Good Coffee

HAMBURGERS

COFFEE THAT HITS THE SPOT

SELF SERVICE

Better BAR-B-Q

OUR COFFEE IS SO GOOD We Always Drink It Ourselves

FOOD Cooked As You Like It

GOOD FOOD SERVED RIGHT

Good FOOD Low PRICES Quick SERVICE

For Those Who Are Fussy ABOUT THEIR FOOD

A Good PLACE To EAT

Golden Brown WHEAT CAKES

Fine Food Quick SERVICE Low PRICES

GOOD FOOD is GOOD HEALTH

Hamburgers THEY'RE A TREAT TO EAT

DINE The BRIGHTEST SPOT in TOWN DANCE

HOT DOGS WITH ALL THE TRIMMINGS

UNUSUAL DISHES

WE PUT THE O.K. IN COOKING

Enjoy Yourself

The Place to REFRESH

FRESH FISH Caught Daily

MEATS Choice Cuts

FISH FRY FRIDAY

None Better COFFEE

FRESH

ELABORATELY and DELICIOUSLY PREPARED CHINESE FOODS we are famous for better CHOW MEIN American Dishes also

FOLLOW the CROWD

Delicious

LIKE MOTHER USED TO MAKE

FROG LEGS

Always Fresh

Good **FOOD**

UNEXCELLED SERVICE

BARBECUED CHICKEN & SPARE RIBS STEAKS CHOPS

HOME COOKING

*F*amous *F*or *F*un and *F*ood

TEACUP READING

TEA ROOM

Chicken **BAR-B-Q**

AIR CONDITIONED

MENU

Real **BAR-B-Q**

FOUNTAIN SPECIALS **TASTY SANDWICHES**

Fountain *Service*

ICE CREAM · SOFT DRINKS

Carbonated **BEVERAGES** *delicious · · Refreshing*

FUR
STORAGE

Call us uk

DRY GOODS

A Complete
Laundry Service

Cleaners
DRY CLEANED
WE CALL & DELIVER

Clean
Rugs
&
Carpets
make
Happier Homes

FUR STORAGE

Furs
STORED
CLEANED
REPAIRED
REMODELED

LINGERIE

GOOD
laundry Work
PROMPTLY
DONE

FURS

FURS

Cleaners — Laundry — Furs

Call on us Laundry *and Washday Worries*

Exclusive LADIES TAILORING

have your Suit Cleaned *today*

Fireproof STORAGE

FUR... HEADQUARTERS REPAIRED... REMODELED... CLEANED... STORED...

A *Careful* LAUNDRY

Come Clean With Us! And Let Us Dye For You

Let Us CLEAN *It*

TRANSFER STORAGE

Our Work is Guaranteed Reliable CLEANERS PICK UP *and* DELIVERY

Radio Shop

Fine Millinery

JUST PHONE US

MAKE EVERY OCCASION A PLEASANT MEMORY with *Gifts* OF DISTINCTION.. *Our Selection is Complete*

A PHONE CALL *Will Bring It*

TABLE *Luxuries*

JEWELRY WATCHES & DIAMONDS WEDDING & GRADUATION GIFTS *on Easy Payment Plan*

free DEMONSTRATION

Make them HAPPY *with* FLOWERS

Buy on our Easy BUDGET PLAN

Cigars Cigarettes

Little Things for a Prettier Home GIFTS

Phone us today!

Newest Creations Jewelry *and* Diamonds WEDDING *and* GRADUATION GIFTS

Good CLEANING gives SMART Appearance

HATS CLEANED BLOCKED

"YOU'RE NEXT" FOR THE BEST HAIRCUT & SHAVE

Oh! Boy! WE CLEAN 'EM

Dress Up

DRY Cleaning

COSTUMES Rented For All Occasions

Cleaned JUST LIKE NEW

CLEANED HATS BLOCKED

Oderless DRY CLEANING

Fine Linens

BARBER SHOP

We APPRECIATE your PATRONAGE

Complete VALET SERVICE

WE ARE TOPS IN DRY CLEANING

LOOK WELL DRESSED Careful CLEANING

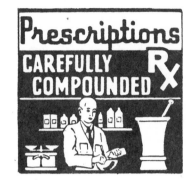

POOL AND BILLIARDS

BOWLING IS HEALTHFUL

BOWL for HEALTH KEEP IN SHAPE

ARCHERY Range TEST YOUR SKILL

ROLLER SKATE for HEALTH

BOWLING BILLIARDS

WE HAVE BOATS to HIRE for PLEASURE · FISHING

RODEO Thrills Galore

For a Real VACATION ON THE LAKE

COME - - - where they really bite

MARINE SUPPLIES

Winter Sports

BOWLING

Right Down Your Alley

RENT a BICYCLE

BICYCLES

It's Fun to RIDE A BIKE

BOWL for health

Learn GOLF

STOP & SOCK

Play GOLF

FOR HEALTH

GOLF LESSONS

IMPROVE YOUR FORM

Calling ALL GOLFERS

PUBLIC FEE COURSE

SPORTING GOODS

BAIT

For all kinds of fishing

VACATION PARADISE

FLY

FOR BUSINESS OR PLEASURE

Relax

AT THE SHORE

TOURISTS
CABINS
MODERN
ALL COMFORTS

The CENTER of VACATION LAND

COTTAGES

Approved
MOTEL
TOURIST HOME
BATH · · PARKING

Horses for Hire

RIDING STABLES

GUEST HOME
Approved by
MOTEL

Dancing

Instructions

Tourists
Camp

Dance
INSTRUCTION
by Experts

Swimming.. Boating.. Fishing..

DRIVE IN

BILLIARDS

water sports

SPORTING GOODS

LIGHT GROCERIES

VACATION CABINS

WE RENT BOATS by the HOUR DAY OR WEEK

Fishing Boating · Swimming

SERVICE Plus QUALITY

SMILING Service

Bowl Your Cares Away

Eat Be Merry Drink

—RIGHT DOWN OUR ALLEY—
BOWLING

WILL CHASE YOUR CARES AWAY

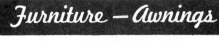

Call Us For **Better Shades**

MODERNIZE **YOUR HOME**

For a better Window Cleaning Service

Improve ADD A ROOM SCREEN UP! ENCLOSE YOUR PORCH *Your* **HOME**

Everything for the Office

Carpets and Linoleums

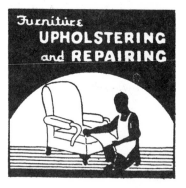

FURNITURE Bought & Sold

New & Used Office **FURNITURE**

Furniture **UPHOLSTERING** and **REPAIRING**

AWNINGS

UPHOLSTERING

Baby **FURNITURE**

CAMERA SUPPLIES

Thank You COME IN AGAIN

Only the best in PHOTO Finishing

Be there with a PORTABLE RADIO

RECORDINGS of your favorite SYMPHONIES

DANCE RECORDS *Latest Releases*

TENTS and AWNINGS

It's so Easy to Learn to play the PIANO

BUY HERE with CONFIDENCE

Records

Musical Instruments

The MUSIC SHOP

For Success
Custom Tailored Clothes

We Give Personal Service

Uniforms MADE TO MEASURE

Fine HABERDASHERY

STYLES for DISCRIMINATING MEN

Complete MEN'S WEAR

Custom Tailoring at Its Best

MERCHANT Tailoring
STYLE VALUE QUALITY

Custom Tailoring at Its Best

Style-Value-Quality

MEN'S FURNISHINGS

Up-To-The-Minute In STYLES

For the Particular Man...

MEN'S & BOYS' WEAR

IT PAYS TO BE WELL GROOMED

MEN'S WEAR

TURKISH

BATHS

SHOES for Men

PHYSICAL CULTURE

Enjoy Life

QUICK SERVICE Shoe REPAIRING

QUALITY and SERVICE is

OUR MOTTO

Fine FOOTWEAR for the Entire Family

Complete FOOTWEAR for MEN

SCIENTIFIC Scalp Treatment

Quality FOOTWEAR

BEAUTY CULTURE

For Particular Women

DRESSES

Fine HOSIERY

BRIDAL SHOP

LINGERIE

CHARM BEAUTY

Fashionable WOMEN'S APPAREL

Latest Creations in DRESSES

Accessories for Lovely Women

Smart HATS

Fine HOSIERY

BUILDING
MATERIAL
New and Used

LANDSCAPING

NURSERY
STOCK

LANDSCAPING

HEATING
STEAM
· HOT
WATER
· HOT
AIR
·

GARDEN TOOLS

PLUMBING
Prompt Service

Everything for the Painter & Decorator

PAINT UP

PLUMBING
Fixtures

HOMES

Wall papers - **PAINTS**
COMPLETE
LINE OF
PAINTERS
SUPPLIES

PLASTER-ING
CEMENT WORK
BRICK LAYING

PAINTERS
DECORATORS

READY MIXED
CONCRETE

HEATING
Air CONDITIONING

General CONTRACTORS

Beautify *Your Home*

This—
HERE LIES MR. PEST AND RELATIVES
NOTE: DEATH BY *Scientific* EXTERMINATION

PROMPT · EFFICIENT
PLUMBING SERVICE

Better ROOFING

Scientific EXTERMINATION

BOILER REPAIRS
Electric & Acetylene Welding

EXTERMINATORS
Reliable Service

SPARTON *Radios*

EVERYTHING ELECTRICAL

SOUND SYSTEMS

NEON *Signs*

MAINTAINED — REPAIRED
MANUFACTURED — ERECTED

FLUORESCENT *Lighting*

• SERVICE
• FIXTURES

RADIOS

all Makes REPAIRED

ELECTRIC REFRIGERATION

MAINTE-
NANCE &
REPAIRS

Smart Economy

To Buy

LONG DISTANCE

RADIO

ELECTRICAL SERVICE

LATEST MODEL RADIOS

On Easy

PAYMENTS

A Complete Line of **FARM** IMPLEMENTS

KEYS OF ALL KINDS

REFRIGERATORS *Easy Terms*

We Repair *Any Make or Model*

WELDING

Hardware TOOLS

See before YOU BUY

REFRIGERATOR *Maintenance*

Enjoy **AUTOMATIC HEAT**

• CONVENIENCE
• COMFORT

With *Uniform* **HEAT**

The BUY OF YOUR LIFE — ELECTRIC

Everything in **HARDWARE**

LOW INTEREST RATES

LOANS

Loans Quickly

LOW INTEREST RATE

NEED MONEY? Loans QUICKLY CONFIDENTIALLY

LOANS

Let Us Help You

Currency EXCHANGE

Cash

WHEN YOU NEED IT

CURRENCY Exchange

AUTO LOANS

CASH

WHEN YOU NEED IT

Complete Home Outfitters

Checks Cashed

MONEY ORDERS

SALARIES BOUGHT

A BANKING Institution " Offering SECURITY and SERVICE

INSURANCE POLICY SICK & ACCIDENT

Guaranteed Protection that's INSURANCE

INSURANCE FOR Financial Independence

We're as near as your TELEPHONE Give us a RING

SERVICE Is our first thought .

Complete . . . . . . HOME FURNISHINGS

INSURANCE Of All Kinds for Financial INDEPENDENCE

PHONE US for PROMPT SERVICE

A phone call will bring RELIABLE HELP

A 24 hour SERVICE

INSURANCE Is your Best PROTECTOR

Drink MILK for HEALTH

Fancy Cakes TASTY PASTRIES

DAIRY PRODUCTS

DAIRY Products BUTTER·EGGS·CHEESE

big or little Orders ARE ALWAYS WELCOME

MILK EGGS BUTTER

FRESH FISH

Potato Chips

Come In YOU'LL ALWAYS FIND SOME HERE

HOME MADE Candies FRESH - PURE

Fruits & VEGETABLES

Fresh Fruits and Vegetables

Luscious **PIES**

A box of good **CANDY** *always makes friends*

**WEDDING &
ANNIVERSARY
CAKES**

Quality ALWAYS FRESH **BAKED GOODS**

fresh Candies

Candy **VENDING MACHINES**

JUST GOOD FOOD **DELICATESSEN**

Choice **MEATS & GROCERIES**

We are featuring **Special Meat Menus** *Delicious* **Attractively Priced** *Everything* in FRESH and CURED MEATS

MEATS POULTRY and FISH

WE PICK UP AND MAKE PROMPT **DELIVERIES**

Choice **MEATS**

OIL *and* **GAS**

COMPLETE SERVICE

TAXI

MODERN SAFE

Dependable

AUTO REPAIRING TOWING

EXPERT SERVICE

AMBULANCE SERVICE

AUTOMOBILE *Accessories*

EVERYTHING FOR YOUR CAR

TOWING

Day & Night Service

WHEEL BALANCING *and...* **ALIGNMENT** *SERVICE*

SCOUT GASOLINE

Quality **AUTO TOPS**

Expert **WORKMANSHIP**

Play Safe! **Call** *a* **TAXI**

GAS & **OIL**

A COMPLETE SERVICE

PROMPT COURTEOUS

TAXI! *Anywhere in Town*

44

CRANK CASE SERVICE TIRES and BATTERIES

GAS AND OIL

OUR BUSINESS IS BATTERIES **PEP 'Em UP** FAST STARTING LONG LIFE

EXPERT **LUBRICATING** SERVICE FOR THE CAR OWNER WHO CARES

GREASING 'EM HELPS AND WE DO A GOOD JOB OF GREASING.

TOWING SERVICE ANYTHING · ANYWHERE ANY TIME NO DISTANCE TOO GREAT

BATTERY *Service* by *Experts*

BATTERY AND **IGNITION** *Service*

Used **Auto Parts**

AT YOUR SERVICE TO HELP — KEEP EM ROLLING

USED CARS DEPENDABLE USED TRUCKS

USED **AUTO PARTS** FOR EVERY MAKE OF CAR

BRAKE SERVICE — *Experts on every make*

USED CARS WITH MANY UNUSED MILES

We Are **Specialists** *In* WIRING IGNITION CABURETION

USED CARS *with* MONEY-BACK *Guarantee*

BATTERIES

Guaranteed Used CARS

Inside **Parking** is the Safest

RENT A CAR *Drive It* YOURSELF

RENT-A-CAR *Commercial Rates*

MOVING LOCAL AND LONG DISTANCE

Ship by Truck

SHIP BY *Truck*

STORAGE MOVING

Everywhere by BUS

We Ship Everywhere

• ECONOMICAL • COMFORTABLE • SAFE GO by BUS

SERVICE *Always!*

Go via Bus Economical Quick Safe

EASY PAYMENTS

WRECKED CARS... made new
BODY and FENDER REPAIRING · PAINTING · GLASS · TOWING ·

CURB SERVICE

How Is Your SPARE

IT PAYS TO HAVE GOOD TIRES
BEWARE of BLOWOUTS from BAD TIRES
for Safety's Sake
LET US REPLACE YOUR WORN TIRES TODAY

USED CARS

Speedy ROAD SERVICE

Superior AUTO REPAIR SERVICE
our Work Guaranteed

No Cash Needed

Auto PAINTING

WE TAKE THE DENTS OUT OF ACCI-DENTS

Cheerful Credit

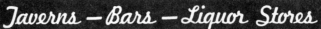

YOU GET THE BEST in WINES & BEERS

BEER Is Good For You

Choice WINES and LIQUORS

WINES for Every Taste

Here 'Tis Come and Get It

STOP here for the BEST BEER in TOWN

Fine WINES & LIQUORS

IF YOU DRIVE YOUR OLD MAN TO DRINK
CLUB 41
DRIVE HIM IN HERE

DOMESTIC & IMPORTED Select WINES

IMPORTED & DOMESTIC WINES LIQUORS for your Pet Drink

CHOICE Liqueurs & WINES

Peppy DRINKS

Here is to YOU & YOURS

THERE'S A TAVERN IN THE TOWN

Beer LIKE OLD TIMES

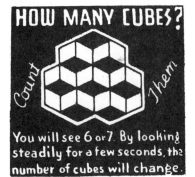

HOW MANY CUBES?

Count Them

You will see 6 or 7. By looking steadily for a few seconds, the number of cubes will change.

Beer on TAP

You are a stranger here but once!

GOOD BEER Tasty SANDWICHES

BEER with Your Lunch

A can go 8 days without a drink but who the wants to be a Camel?

U R ALWAYS WELCOME

WHERE GOOD FELLOWS get TOGETHER

Dine Dance

The Joyous SPOT in town

DRINK & SING DINE AND DANCE

COCKTAIL Lounge

ENTERTAINMENT DINE DANCE

COCKTAIL LOUNGE

We don't hold you up here

EXOTIC · DANCERS

Skol

OH BOY WHAT A FLOOR SHOW

Cocktail LOUNGE

COCKTAILS ★ FOOD ★ GAYETY

WE KEEP YOU IN GOOD SPIRITS

WE DELIVER to YOUR DOOR

Kold Beer In
Kans
Kegs
Kases

Cut Rate — WINES LIQUORS •••• BEER
All Favorite Brands

WORLD'S FINEST
BEER AND ALE

Wines Liquors Beers
We Deliver

Cool Off with Beer

Our Drinks have OOMPH

WINES DRUGS BEERS LIQUORS

DRINKS

WHERE SMART PEOPLE MEET
COCKTAIL HOUR

We Aim To Please

LADIES INVITED

DRUNK

NOT DRUNK IS HE WHO FROM THE FLOOR CAN RISE AGAIN AND DRINK ONCE MORE

BUT DRUNK IS HE WHO PROSTRATE LIES AND CANNOT EITHER DRINK OR RISE

Call Again

BEER

DRINK UP

GESUNDHEIT

The Brewery needs the Barrels.

DRINKS TO·SUIT·A Queens TASTE

HURRY BACK

SANDWICHES

You'll enjoy our BEER and SANDWICHES

You'll Like Our BEER

Here is to you and you and You!

Bottoms Up

DRINK UP

A Complete Line of JEWELRY

The PERFECT GIFT Your PHOTOGRAPH

SCIENTIFIC WATCH REPAIRS

Sympathetic SERVICE

JEWELRY for the Entire Family

WHEN WORDS FAIL YOU "Say it with flowers" Flowers FOR ALL OCCASIONS

FLOWERS For Every Occasion

Say it with Flowers

YOUR INTEREST IS THE HEART of Our BUSINESS

Say It With Flowers

Quality THAT WILL PLEASE YOU

Chicken **DINNERS**

OUR BARGAINS ARE WORTH FIGHTING FOR

I'm On the Menu

SHOES FOR THE ENTIRE FAMILY

Start some monkey business — If you want to know who's boss

LIMP IN Leap Out

End **WASHDAY WORRIES**

Make our phone line your clothes line

We Shine

For MEN **BARBER** for WOMEN

A WORLD OF VALUES

PRIVATE BOOTHS COMFORTABLE · COZY

Where Your Pennies **HAVE MORE CENTS**

Let us do the hurrying for you

LET US HELP YOU SAVE

For CUT PRICES

A Good Place To Buy

Look your Best

WE'LL MEND ANYTHING BUT A BROKEN HEART

24 HOUR Service

WE PUT THE SERVE IN SERVICE

FOLLOW the CROWD

COMPLETE SERVICE

YES SIR! WE ALWAYS LEAD — "HOW DOES HE DO IT?" OTHERS FOLLOW Why Not TRY US

COAST to COAST

PLUS Quality Our MOTTO

ALL WE ASK IS A TRIAL YOU BE THE JUDGE

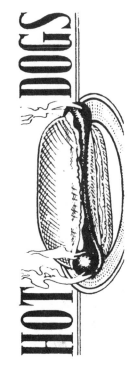

PLUMBING prompt Service Call us

FUNERAL HOME NO EXTRA CHARGE FOR USE OF CHAPEL

FUNERAL CHAPEL *of Unusual Charm & Dignity.*

STEAM FITTING THAT FITS

PURE MILK YOUR BEST FOOD! *Every one* NEEDS A PINT A DAY

FUNERAL *Directors* *Offering a Service Carefully planned and Reasonably Priced*

TRY OUR MILK and **DAIRY PRODUCTS** *Be Sure of Quality.*

WHEN WORDS FAIL YOU **CALL US** WE'LL "EXPRESS" IT

We Appreciate your Patronage

We Do SMALL THINGS BIG

We have the KEY to Greater SAVINGS

YOU CAN HAVE MY SHARE - I KNOW WHAT HAPPENS TO YOU FAT GUYS

For Better Eyesight OPTICIAN

You'll REMEMBER us for VALUE SERVICE QUALITY PRICE

A phone call will bring RELIABLE HELP

Carnival Time

WE AIM TO PLEASE

MERRY XMAS

SEASONS GREETINGS

Merry Christmas

Everything for the
TRAVELER

America
for
AMERICANS

WHERE GOOD FELLOWS
GET TOGETHER

24 hour
WRECKER
SERVICE

U U U B
may belong *to many* ♣
may wear *many* ♦
may have a *big* ♥
BUT you don't *need a* ♠
TO DIG UP OUR LOCATION
SEE OTHER SIDE

An
American
for the People

DONT START
SOMETHING YOU
CANT
FINISH

Health
is
Wealth

Buy
Here
YOUR
CREDIT
IS GOOD

QUALITY
AND
SERVICE
FIRST

MULTIGRAPHING
MIMEOGRAPHING
FOLDING
ADDRESSING
MAILING
A Complete
LETTER SERVICE

RADIATORS

A SNACK OR A SACK

Quality MEATS

TRY OUR Delicious BAR-B-Q "The Flavor is the Thing"

MOST POPULAR PLACE IN TOWN

YOU ARE A STRANGER HERE BUT ONCE

Your Favorite SPOT

PRIVATE BOOTHS COMFORTABLE • COZY

DINNERS ARE DELIGHTFUL HERE! Food for Particular People..

CHOP SUEY

Just Like Mother Used to Cook

The "Ah's" Have it

Better BAR-B-Q

Genuine MEXICAN Dishes